FIRST GUITAR TUTOR

TERENCE ASHLEY

Text adapted by STEPHEN COLE

THIS IS A CARLTON BOOK

Design copyright © 2003 Carlton Publishing Group
Text copyright © 2003 Terence Ashley

This edition published in 2004 by Carlton Books Ltd
A Division of the Carlton Publishing Group
20 Mortimer Street
London
W1T 3JW

First published in 2003

A CIP catalogue for this book is available from the British Library.

ISBN 1 84442 507 X

Text adaptation: Stephen Cole
Project Editor: Amie McKee
Design: Barbara Zuñiga
Picture research: Steve Behan
Production: Lucy Woodhead

Contents page

Introducing the guitar

The guitar is without a doubt the instrument at the heart of most of the popular music of the twentieth century—and you've picked this book up because YOU want to play it.

Our aim is to provide the basic ingredients to let YOU think, act, and play for yourself. Every one of you will have different needs, goals, dreams, and musical aptitudes. For some, being able to strum the chords of a few songs will be more than enough; others may want to play heavy-metal solos at supersonic speeds. Whatever your reasons for wanting to play, the guitar is a truly great tool for expressing and communicating your own musical creativity.

It wouldn't be fair, though, to get through this introduction without uttering the dreaded "P-word." As with any learning process, you only get to be good by PRACTICING. Sadly, there is no short-cut to having your fingers "learn," for example, chords and scales—and unless you are planning a radical overhaul of the basic principles of music, you're going to need both of these. There will be times when this can be frustrating, especially on those occasions when your hands fail to live up to the expectations of your mind.

The only advice I can give here is to take it slowly, and try to keep yourself mentally focused on your ultimate aim. Work methodically through each lesson, and don't move on until you have mastered the last one. And if you think that idea sucks, remember that every guitar hero on the planet has had to pass through the same learning experience—so you're in good company!

But no matter how great the challenge, never let it become torture. The time you spend doing anything should be enjoyable, otherwise it's just not worth bothering. As the legendary Les Paul told me a few years ago: "You don't WORK the guitar, you PLAY it." So with those wise words in mind, get ready to have some fun!

A quick note for left-handers: while many classic guitars are available in mirror-image left-handed models, some players find it easier—and cheaper—to buy a standard model and restring it in reverse. Find out more from your local music store when choosing your guitar.

Watch out for us inside—the **plucky picks**! Well, some people call us **plectrums**...

Although technically, we should be called **plectra**...

Terence Ashley

Well, *technically* we shouldn't be able to **speak**. So be quiet and let's get on with it!

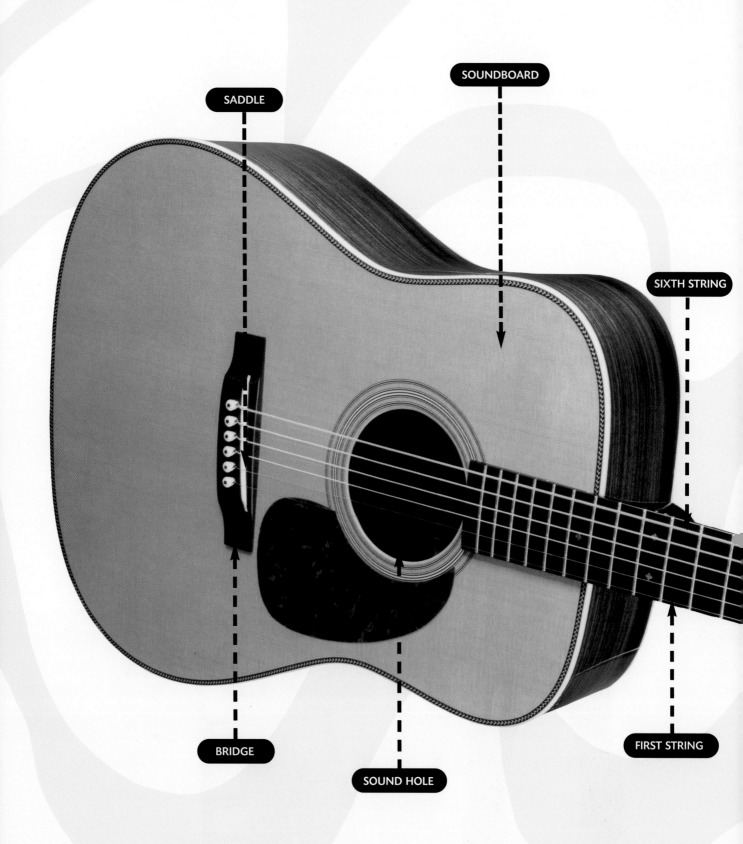

SADDLE

SOUNDBOARD

SIXTH STRING

BRIDGE

SOUND HOLE

FIRST STRING

How does an acoustic guitar work?

You make music on a guitar by striking the strings. This sets the strings vibrating. Their vibrations disturb the surrounding air, creating a kind of energy. By passing this energy into the guitar's soundbox via the bridge saddle—the point where each string comes into direct contact with the guitar's body—an audible sound is created. The vibrations of each string create a different sound, so by playing them in different combinations you can make tunes!

The sound produced by any acoustic guitar depends on:

1 what it is made from
2 how it is designed

These materials and design play a very important role in the volume and quality of the sound. A hunt round a typical music store will reveal several different guitar designs—because not all players like the same kind of sound and some instruments are better suited to certain styles of music than others. And, of course, no two guitars will ever sound *exactly* the same because they are made from different pieces of wood!

The soundboards of most quality instruments are made from spruce…

Cheaper guitars use plywood or laminated timbers, which may give a muddier sound—so beware!

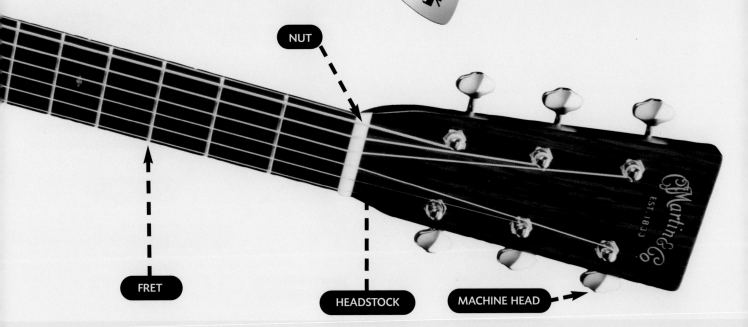

NUT

FRET

HEADSTOCK

MACHINE HEAD

Guitars get LOUDER!

By the 1920s guitars were commonly used in jazz and dance bands, often in place of the more traditional banjo. However, during this time the guitar's naturally low volume, compared to the other acoustic instruments, meant that it was usually used only to provide a rhythmic backing. Then some smart dude developed a special pickup, which was fitted to the acoustic instrument to magnify the soundwaves. These soundwaves were channeled through a loudspeaker, which boosted the volume greatly. Suddenly the guitar could really be heard—and music would never be the same.

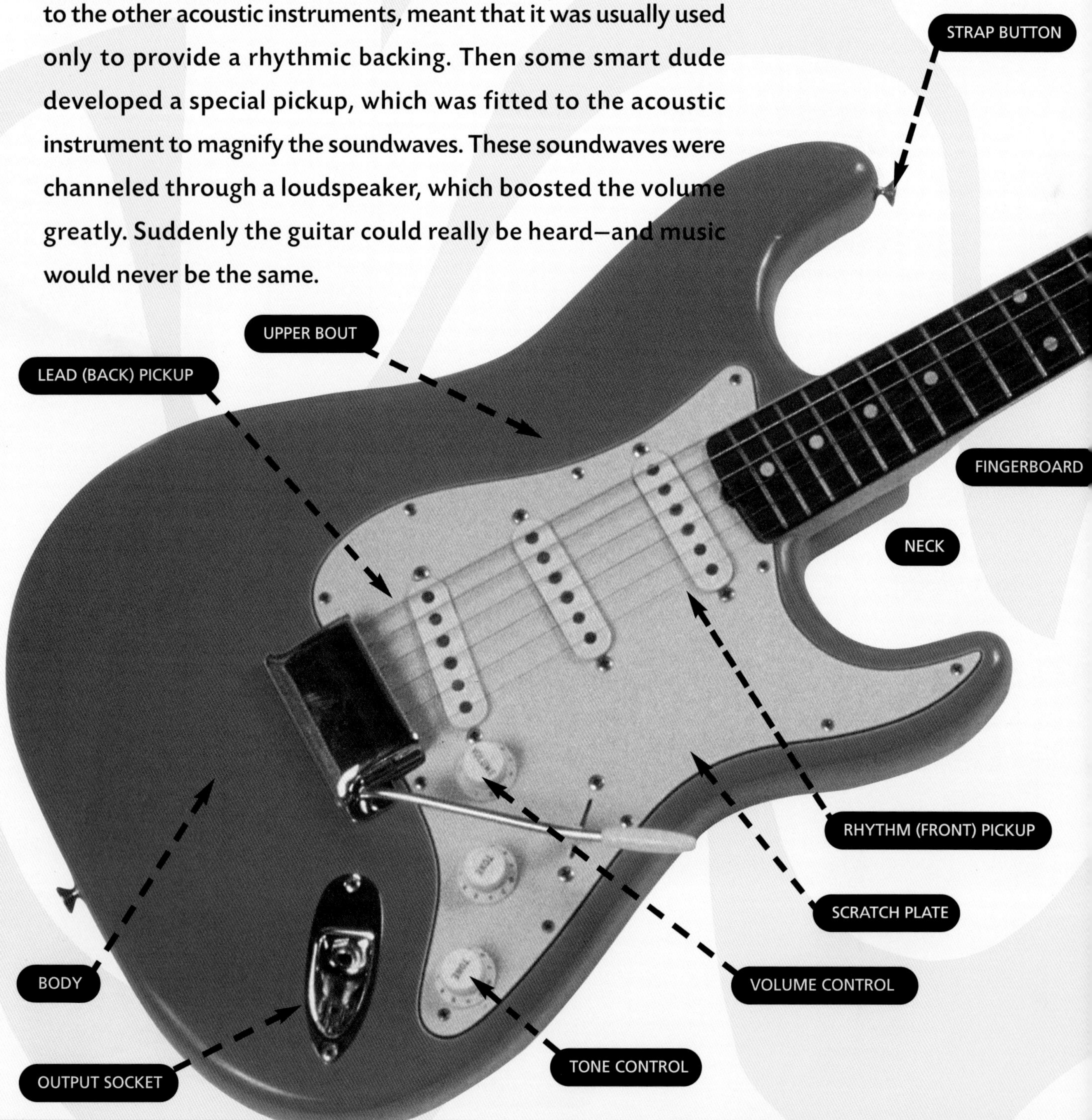

STRAP BUTTON

UPPER BOUT

LEAD (BACK) PICKUP

FINGERBOARD

NECK

RHYTHM (FRONT) PICKUP

SCRATCH PLATE

BODY

VOLUME CONTROL

OUTPUT SOCKET

TONE CONTROL

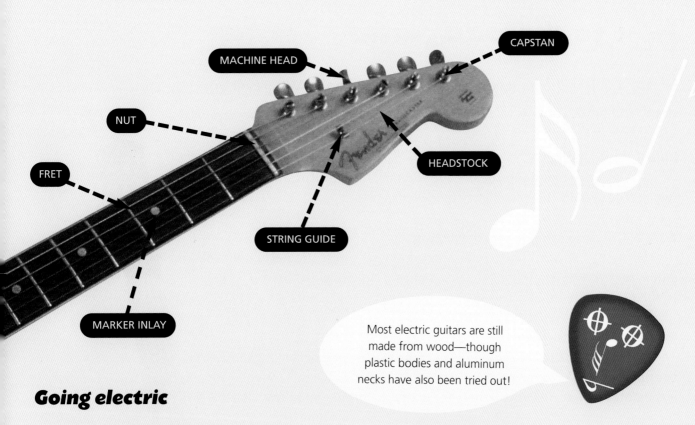

MACHINE HEAD

CAPSTAN

NUT

FRET

HEADSTOCK

STRING GUIDE

MARKER INLAY

Most electric guitars are still made from wood—though plastic bodies and aluminum necks have also been tried out!

Going electric

There was one big problem with fitting pickups to an acoustic guitar—if the amplifier volume was too great, the sound from the loudspeaker would cause the body of the guitar to vibrate, producing a howling noise known as feedback. To reduce the guitar's capacity for vibration, manufacturers decided to make the body of electric guitars solid. There's no need for a soundhole on a true electric guitar—the sound is carried electronically via a lead through to the amplifier.

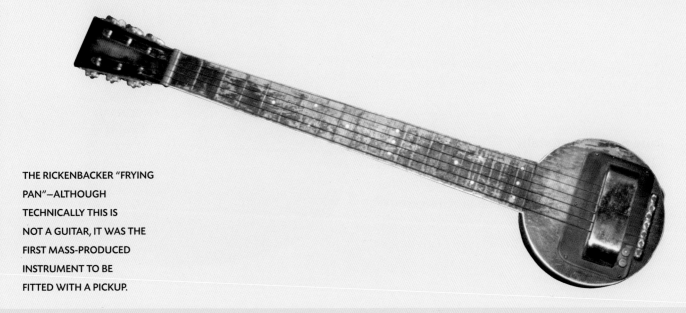

THE RICKENBACKER "FRYING PAN"—ALTHOUGH TECHNICALLY THIS IS NOT A GUITAR, IT WAS THE FIRST MASS-PRODUCED INSTRUMENT TO BE FITTED WITH A PICKUP.

How to choose a guitar

Buying a guitar can be a nerve-wracking experience. Wherever you shop, and whoever you take with you, here are some top tips:

Rule 1 Buy quality
It is easy to find something cheap—but you may find it turns out to be hard to play. Always buy the best guitar that you can afford.

Rule 2 Check for fingerboard warping
A guitar with a warped fingerboard is bad news. To test the neck, hold the guitar as if you were aiming a rifle, and align your eye with the top surface of the neck. If the top of the fingerboard seems twisted, DON'T BUY IT!

Rule 3 Check intonation
The note on the 12th fret should ALWAYS be exactly one octave higher than the open string. Ask someone in the store to demonstrate this for you—and if the notes do not match, ask them to rectify the problem for you.

Rule 4 Check the action
Look at the distance between the top of the 12th fret and the bottom of the string. This height is known as the "action." A low action means that the strings are closer to the frets— this is good because your fingers don't have to press hard to play a note.

Rule 5 Check the machine heads
The machine heads—or "tuners", as they are also known— are the mechanisms on the headstock at the top of the neck that control the tension of each string. If they turn too easily, the strings may slip, making the guitar difficult to keep in tune.

Rule 6 Check sustain
The quality of sustain—the time a note rings naturally before it fades out—differs between instruments. Play every note on the fingerboard, to ensure that all notes sustain equally. Avoid instruments on which "dead" notes can be heard.

If you know anyone who already plays guitar, why not take them with you? They've been through all this before!

Rule 7 Check the pickups

Plug an electric guitar into an amplifier. Twang each string. If the volume varies greatly, the height of the pickups needs to be adjusted. Ask someone in the store if they can do something about this.

Rule 8 Check for noise

With the guitar still plugged in, stand it close to the amplifier and listen to the sound. It should be silent. Unpleasant, whistling feedback means you may have problems when playing at high volumes.

Rule 9 Know what you're hearing

Make sure that the amplifier in the store is not enhancing the quality of the guitar. Ask for any effects to be switched off so that you hear only the amplified guitar.

Rule 10 Enjoy

Every guitar has a sound and feel of its own. It's important that you feel happy with the instrument—this relationship will play a major part in your development as a guitarist!

Back to basics

If you are completely new to the idea of written music, the following pages will give you a good idea of what it's all about. If it seems a bit mysterious at first, don't panic—you'll soon get your head round it!

Naming the notes

There are 12 different notes—these can be seen easily on the diagram of a piano keyboard below. The difference (or **interval**) between each note is called a **half step**.

The white notes on the keyboard are named from A to G. Each of the black notes can have two possible names. Sometimes they can be seen as a "sharpened" version of the note to their immediate left. In such cases they

take that note name, followed by a **sharp** symbol (♯). In other cases they may be seen as a "flattened" version of the note to the immediate right, in which case they take that note name followed by a **flat** symbol (♭).

After every 12 notes, the sequence of lettering repeats itself; if you find the note C on a piano keyboard, the same note—lower or higher—can be heard 12 half steps either side of that note. An interval of 12 half steps is referred to as an **octave**.

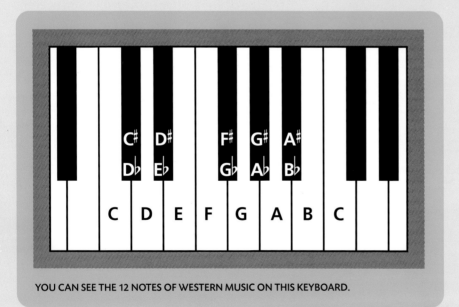

YOU CAN SEE THE 12 NOTES OF WESTERN MUSIC ON THIS KEYBOARD.

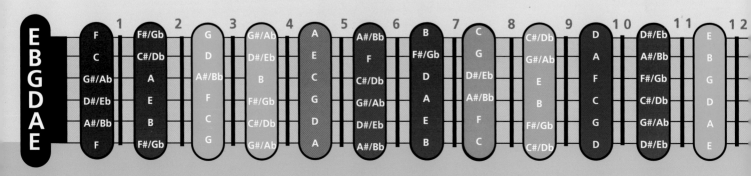

Know your notation

Music is traditionally written out on a set of five lines known as a **staff**—or **staves** when there's more than one.

The guitar's range is limited to four octaves, and the music for it is written on a single treble staff—which is why the symbol of a treble clef (𝄞) can be seen before the notes.

For a treble clef, the notes *on* the lines are E, G, B, D and F. The notes *between* the lines are F, A, C, and E. The diagram below makes this clear. Flat or sharp notes appear on the line after which they are named (so, for instance, E♭ would appear on the E line) with either a ♭ or ♯ symbol appearing alongside.

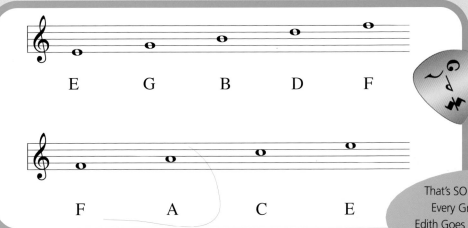

E   G   B   D   F

F   A   C   E

A special rhyme can help you remember the notes on the line! Every Good Boy Deserves Favors!

That's SO boring! Check these:
Every Groovy Bird Digs Fish!
Edith Goes Bananas Down Florida!
Eat Good Bacon, Don't Forget!

Guitar TABs

A complementary form of written music often used for the guitar is the TAB system. This is simply a six-line grid in which each line represents a string, from top to bottom. A number written on a line is an instruction to play a specific fret.

This has an advantage over notes on staves in that it tells you exactly which fret on which to play a note.

The full range of notes along the fingerboard is shown on the diagram below.

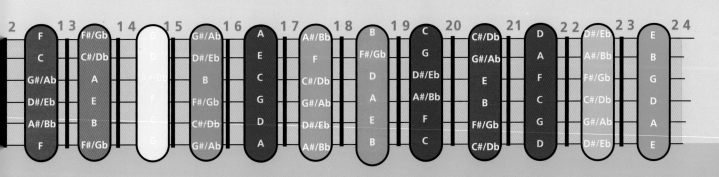

Sitting or standing?

Before you start to play it's important that you feel relaxed and comfortable holding your instrument. The way you play depends a bit on the type of music you play. Generally, classical, folk and flamenco players are seen seated, whereas most rock and country players perform in a standing position with the guitar supported by a shoulder strap.

Take a seat!

Practicing for any length of time can place quite a strain on mind and body. It's important you feel comfortable while you play.

If you've got an acoustic guitar, why not take a seat? Remember, though, not every seating surface is good for playing the guitar. You should choose a sturdy stool or upright chair. The floor on which the left-foot is positioned also needs to be firm. Desk chairs aren't much use since the arms will just get in the way. Nor is a sofa or bed a good idea! They may be nice and comfy but you'll find it hard to hold the guitar in the correct position— and this can encourage bad habits.

THAT'S THE WAY TO DO IT! SIT YOUR WAY TO SUCCESS!

Once you've found your perfect chair, just follow these three simple steps!

1 Rest the guitar on your right thigh.
2 Support the neck with the left hand so that it stays in a broadly horizontal position.
3 Move your right hand down to the strings, like you're about to play. You should find now that the body of the guitar is held in place by the inside of the right arm.

How does that feel?

Take a stand!

To play the guitar in the standing position you will need a shoulder strap. Almost any strap you see in a music store will be fine—but paying a little more money for a good-quality leather strap is usually a worthwhile investment. It should last you a lifetime!

With a shoulder strap in place, the guitar should hang naturally against your body, leaving both arms free to move comfortably. Ideally, the neck of the guitar should be held at the angle shown in the picture. Then, adjust the strap until the guitar is held at the correct height—a good rule for a beginner is to ensure that the bridge hangs at about the same height as your waist.

Of course, you'll see a lot of rock and pop stars perform on stage with extremely low-slung instruments. While this may look cooler than the standard pose, it will make learning more difficult. So be patient—you'll find you develop your own way of holding and playing the guitar, as time goes by!

BE UPSTANDING... AND FIND
YOUR OWN STYLE!

Take care what you wear when you're playing. If your sleeves are too loose they can drag against the strings...

... and metal buttons, jewelry and zippers can all catch the body of the guitar. As well as making a nasty noise, this can scratch your guitar!

Left-hand techniques

Notes are played when the fingers of the left hand force the strings down between the frets on the fingerboard. Making sure you have the correct left-hand posture is important—if you start with bad habits it is very difficult to put them right later on.

The classical left-hand technique has the thumb held against the back of the neck of the guitar at all times. For correct classical posture the thumb must be kept perfectly straight.

Many self-taught players can be seen sliding the left-hand thumb around the neck so that it rests along the edge of the fingerboard. Classical teachers frown on this as a bad habit—but some players find it easier and more comfortable.

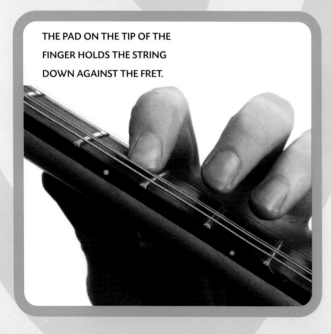

THE PAD ON THE TIP OF THE FINGER HOLDS THE STRING DOWN AGAINST THE FRET.

Don't fret about fretting!

Getting good at fretting is a vital part of developing your left hand in its tough new job! The tip of the finger should fall immediately behind the fret. If it is held too far back the string may buzz against the fret. If it is too close to the fret, the string will be muted.

To avoid accidentally muting the other strings when fretting a note, all of the fingers should be kept upright at right angles to the strings and those not being used should be held clear.

Guitarists who play without a pick often grow the nails of their right hand long enough for them to be able to strike the strings.

So, the next time you see someone with short nails on one hand and long nails on the other you can guess why!

⌢ F I N G E R N A I L S ⌢

It is almost impossible to play the guitar if the fingernails on your left hand are too long. Test their length by bringing them down vertically onto a table top. If the tip of the nail touches the surface before the pad of the finger—get out the nailclippers!

WORKING THE LEFT HAND

These two exercises should get you used to the idea of playing notes with the different fingers of your left hand. You will see that the notes in each of the exercises are the same notes played on different strings: in exercise 1 you are always playing the note C; in exercise 2, the note G.

In each case you must press the finger between the frets and sound the string with your right hand. You can use either your fingers or a pick—only make sure that you use just enough pressure on the fingerboard so that the note played is clear. If you press too lightly the sound will be muted; too hard and your fingers will get tired, and you may develop blisters.

Stop playing as soon as your fingers get tired or start to hurt. It will take a while before your fingers become used to pressing down nylon or metal strings.

Exercise 1

String	Fret	Finger
1	8	1st
2	1	1st
3	5	2nd
4	10	3rd
5	3	4th
6	8	4th

Exercise 2

String	Fret	Finger
1	3	1st
2	8	1st
3	12	2nd
4	5	3rd
5	10	4th
6	3	4th

Get in tune!

The first rule of playing the guitar—whatever your style of music—is to get it in tune. One of the most difficult parts of learning any instrument is developing the ability to hear tiny variations in pitch. Not everyone is gifted with a "musical ear," but it is something that can be learned and improved just like any other skill—so don't stress if it's something that doesn't come naturally to you.

Pitch battle!

Although guitar strings are always the same length in relation to one another, each open string is of a different gauge, or thickness. The fattest strings give the lowest notes and the thinnest strings the highest. The pitch of a string is altered by turning the machine head—this is how you tune up your guitar.

The only truly accurate way of tuning your guitar is to use an independent reference tone. An electronic keyboard or well-tuned piano will also do the trick, but buying a guitar tuner is probably the easiest way of getting in tune.

Get into the habit of making sure that your guitar is in tune every time you pick it up to play.

Take care in deciding which one you go for! If you're playing electric, you simply have to plug your lead into the tuner and follow the simple instructions. If you're playing an acoustic guitar, make sure you get a tuner with a microphone built in—otherwise it will be useless to you!

MANY CHEAP AND RELIABLE ELECTRONIC TUNERS ARE ON THE MARKET.

TUNE UP BY TURNING THE GUITAR'S MACHINE HEADS UNTIL THE DESIRED PITCH OF EACH STRING IS REACHED.

THE NOTES

The six guitar strings are tuned according to specific musical intervals. Put simply, that means that from top to bottom, the string notes are E, B, G, D, A and E. This diagram shows the relationship between the strings of the guitar and the notes of a keyboard.

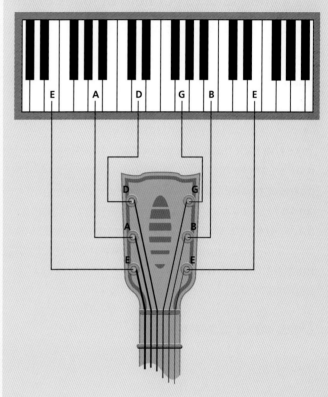

Don't pluck the strings too hard with your right hand when tuning, This can cause the sound to distort, which will make the tuning process more difficult to control.

Take your pick!

For the guitar string to make a sound, it has to be struck by the right hand. Most players use a pick. This is a triangular object, usually made from plastic or tortoiseshell, which is held between the first finger and the thumb of the right hand. There are lots of different types of picks available. As a new player, it's a good idea to get hold of loads of them. You'll quickly find which one you prefer—and you'll be OK should you happen to lose one or two!

Ooooh! I love being talked about!

Hold it!

Take the pick between thumb and forefinger. Hold it at an angle of 90° to the body of the guitar and parallel to the strings. The finger grip should be quite relaxed but tight enough so that it doesn't move around while you are playing. As you strike the string you should swivel the wrist and forearm, moving the joints of the thumb and fingers. It's important that this should be a flowing movement.

Ups and downs

There are two ways to strike a string with a pick—downstrokes and upstrokes. A downstroke is made by taking the tip of the pick above the string and pushing down. The upstroke is the reverse—the tip is placed below the string and pulled up. Each method has its own symbol, making it possible to indicate in written music the type of stroke that should be played. This notation is usually found above the notes on the staff.

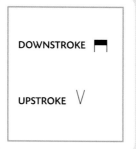

DOWNSTROKE

UPSTROKE ∨

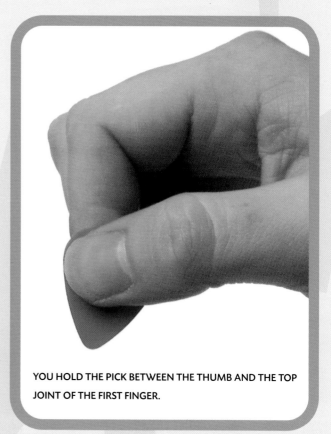

YOU HOLD THE PICK BETWEEN THE THUMB AND THE TOP JOINT OF THE FIRST FINGER.

Exercise time!

The exercises below will set you on your way to mastering the pick. Don't panic—you'll only be picking open strings. This will allow you to concentrate fully on the right-hand technique without having to worry about fretting notes with the left hand. Try to keep the speed at which you play the notes and the strength with which you hit the strings consistent.

Check back to pages 12 and 13 if you're not sure how to read the staves below!

Exercise 1

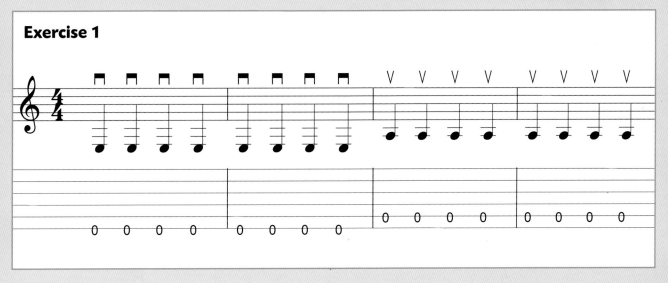

Exercise 2

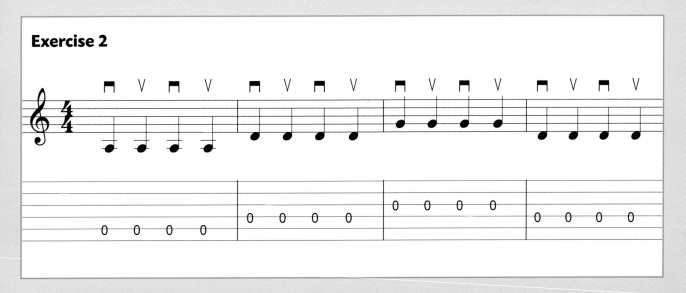

Pick some more!

Here are two more exercises to help you practice your picking powers! Still just the open strings to worry about for now.

Remember! Take a break if your fingers are getting sore.

Exercise 3

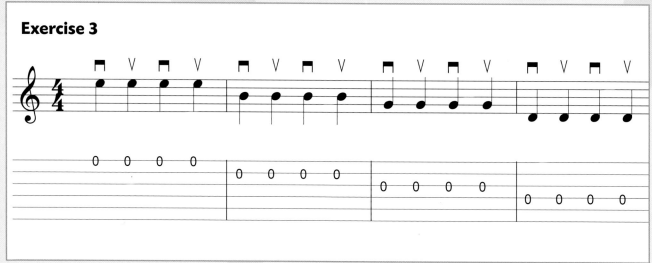

Exercise 4

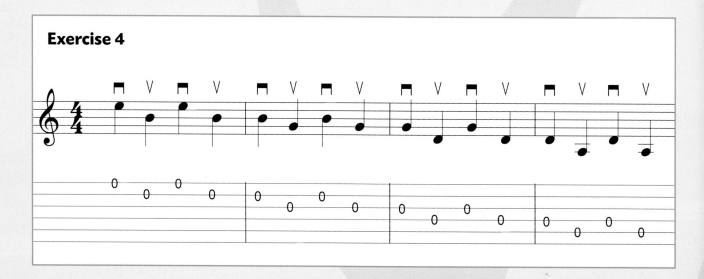

No sweating—get fretting!

These two exercises include some simple fretting on the same string. It may seem daunting, but just take each exercise slowly at first. Try tapping your foot or counting aloud to keep time. Don't worry if you go wrong time after time. If you keep with it, you'll find it gets easier and easier... until suddenly you're note perfect!

Exercise 5

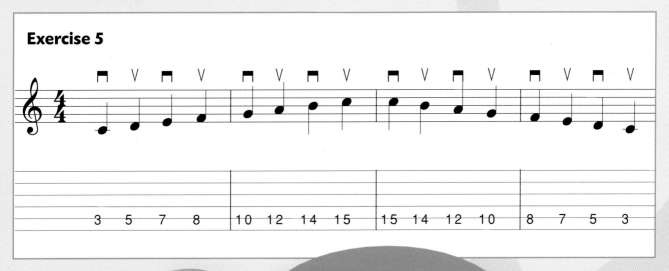

Don't forget—the numbers refer to the fret you should play to make each note. You can refresh your fretting memory by turning to the diagram on pages 12 and 13!

Exercise 6

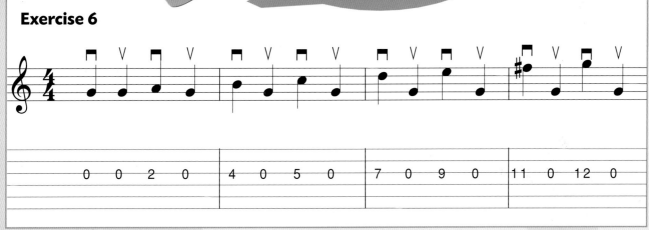

Play these tunes till you're sick to death of them! Remember, they're preparing you for bigger and better things!

Fingerpicking good!

Fingerpicking is used in classical, flamenco and a wide variety of folk and country styles. Whilst there are a great many variations used within these different styles, the most commonly found technique uses the individual fingers of the right hand to play specific strings.

Caught right-handed!

Classical guitarists are trained to strike the strings with their fingernails rather than the pads of the fingers. This is fairly uncommon in other styles of music. The most common alternative is the "clawhammer" style used by steel-string players. You can see the differences in the pictures below. The classical position rests the inside of the forearm at the upper edge of the guitar's body. The clawhammer method rests the palm of the hand on the bridge.

THE CLASSICAL HAND POSITION.

Picks, fingers or both?

Unless you're playing classical or flamenco guitar, the decision as to whether you play with a pick or the fingers is up to you. In country and jazz, the most accomplished guitarists are skilled in either technique. Rock and pop music is dominated by plectrum players, and it's fair to say that the use of some heavy-duty electronic effects makes subtle nuances in picking difficult to spot. There are no real hard-and-fast rules—try out both ways and see how you get on!

THE CLAWHAMMER HAND POSITION.

Pick an exercise!

Once again, the exercises across the page are largely based on playing the open strings. Focus on that right hand! The first exercise uses just the thumb playing the three bass strings. Keep the thumb straight at all times—the playing action should come from the thumb joint, not the knuckle. In exercise 2, use your first, second and third fingers to play the first, second and third strings. Try to strike the notes evenly. The final two exercises bring the thumb and fingers together. To play exercise 4, you have to pick two strings at once, so good luck with that one!

Exercise 1

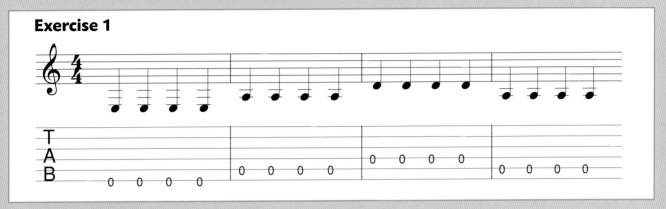

Exercise 2

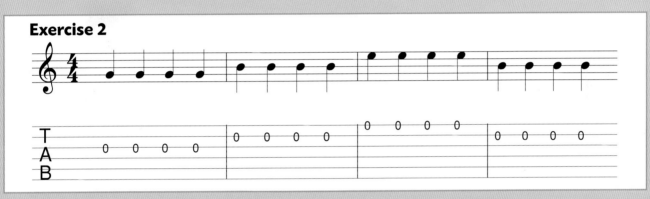

Exercise 3

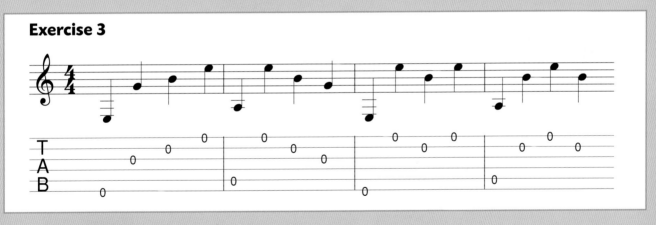

Exercise 4

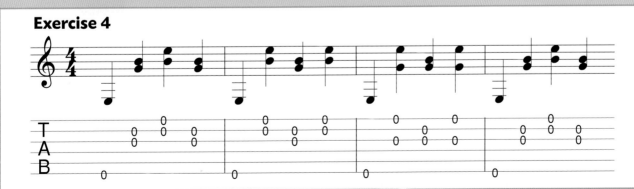

Strike a chord!

Chords are a central part of all guitar-based music. A chord is the effect of three or more notes being played at the same time. Chords are formed on the guitar by pressing the fingers of the left hand onto specific positions on the fingerboard. Once you get started you will quickly become familiar with the basic chord shapes, and understand how they sound in relation to one another.

E-asy does it!

You're now ready to make what will hopefully be your first recognizably musical sound—an E major chord!

The easiest chords to learn are known as open-string chords. They are called this because they can be formed by using a combination of unfretted strings, and the first two or three frets along the fingerboard. The E major chord is particularly special, since the basic shape can be moved along the fingerboard to create a wide range of different chords.

Fretting The Chord

Here are four easy steps to playing an open E major chord. Take it slowly, one step at a time. Your fingers are likely to feel extremely uncomfortable to begin with. Don't worry—this is totally normal.

1 Place the 2nd finger of your left hand on the 2nd fret of the 5th string.
2 Place the 3rd finger of your left hand on the 2nd fret of the 4th string.
3 Place the index finger of your left hand on the 1st fret of the 3rd string.
4 With a pick in your right hand, strum across all six strings.

Congratulations—you've just played your very first chord!

HERE'S HOW YOUR FINGERS SHOULD LOOK WHEN PLAYING E MAJOR.

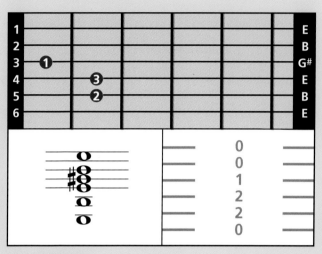

E major

⌒READING CHORD DIAGRAMS⌒

The chord diagrams shown throughout the book are simple to understand. Think of each diagram as if you were looking over the fretboard of a guitar. The dots placed between frets on the strings show where to place your fingers. The number on each dot tells you which finger you should use (1 through 4 represent the index finger to the little finger). If no number is shown, fretting the note is optional. Beside the chord chart you will find the note names of each string. If the note is marked "X," then the string should not be played. A note name shown in brackets also indicates that the note is optional.

Stick with it!

Hopefully you found playing E major majorly E-asy! If not, just keep practicing. The good news is that the simplest chords in music are also the most commonly used. Once you've learned to play the chords in this book pretty well, you will probably be able to play a lot of your favorite songs!

The E major chord is an example of a triad, because it's made up of three different notes. Over the page you'll find more triads to play!

Three chord tricks

The next two chords you will learn about are A major and D major. These chords are closely related to E major, which you have just played. Some of the greatest songs in many styles of music have been written using only this three-chord trick.

A-mazing A major!

When you play the A major chord, the 6th string is optional—the note is shown alongside the chord diagram in brackets. This bottom E is correct musically, but because it is lower in pitch than the chord's root note, it can make the overall sound of the chord seem wrong.

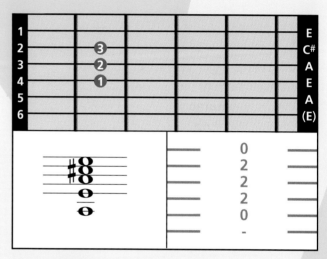

A major

HERE'S HOW YOUR FINGERS SHOULD LOOK WHEN PLAYING A MAJOR.

D-elightful D major!

A D major chord can be played in different ways. You can either:

1 ignore the bottom two strings, and only play the notes of the other four.

2 include the 5th string—even though the note A is lower in pitch than the root D, the chord still generally sounds pretty cool played this way.

3 bring your thumb around the back of the neck to play the F# on the 2nd fret of the 1st string. This is frowned upon by teachers, but has been used by many guitar legends over the years!

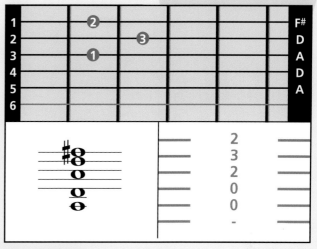

D major

HERE'S HOW YOUR FINGERS SHOULD LOOK WHEN PLAYING D MAJOR.

Think you're ready to change between these different chords now? Then turn over the page!

Changing chords

You've learned your first three chords... Now it's time
for the exciting part—to put them all together!

Getting tough

The exercises shown below will help you to get
used to the idea of moving around between the
three chord shapes you have just learned. Don't
worry about keeping time for the moment, just
concentrate on getting your fretting spot on.

If you are an absolute beginner, THIS WILL BE A
TOUGH EXERCISE. It's well worth concentrating
on this section for a while before you move on to
the other chords. Try not to be discouraged if it
doesn't come easily. Just remember—every guitar
player in the world has been here at some stage.
And you can bet that they found it just as difficult!

Here are those chord diagrams
again so you don't have to
keep flipping the page!

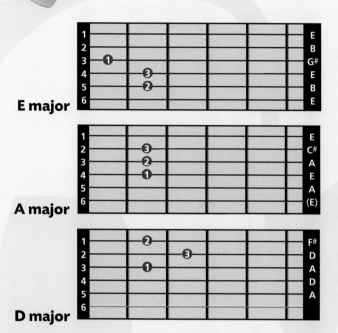

E major

A major

D major

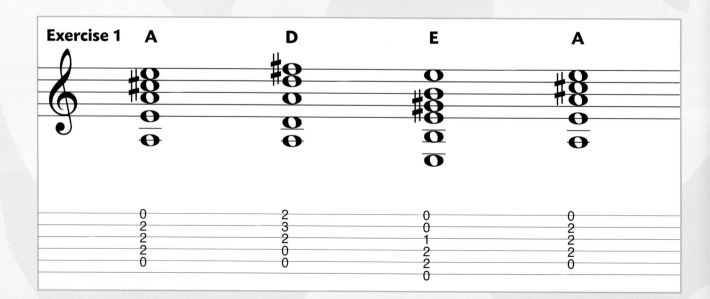

Exercise 2

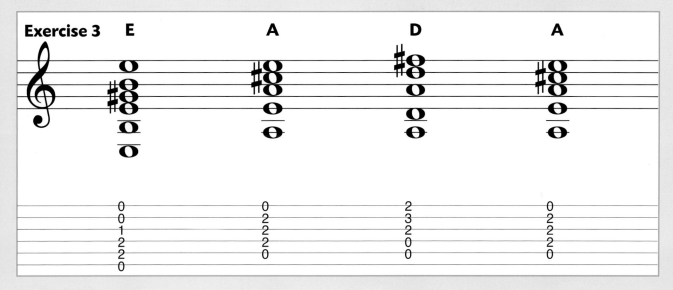

Exercise 3

Exercise 4

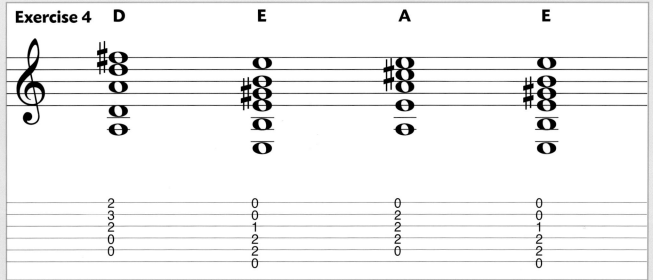

More open-string chords!

Here you go... presented for your playing delight!

Now I'm really starting to warm up!

G-lorious G major!

C-elebrated C major!

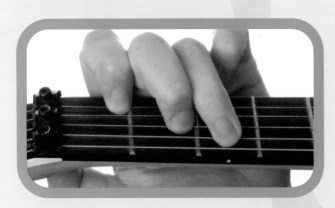

F-antastic F major!

Minor matters

Now we'll move on to minor chords. A minor chord is created by "flattening" the third note of a major triad—that means reducing it by a half step, or one fret on the fingerboard.

E-lectric E minor!

A-stounding A minor!

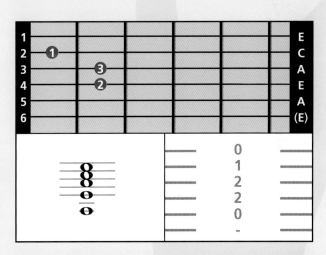

D-eafening D minor!

Chord fluency

The next set of exercises brings together some of the new chords you've been practicing. Try to play each exercise as smoothly as possible—and this time, see if you can begin to keep time. As you play, count out aloud: "One-and-two-and-three-and-four-and," striking a new chord each time you reach "One." Or, if you find counting and playing at the same time is tricky, you can play along with a beat box—just be careful not to set the tempo too fast!

These four chord sequences are "turnarounds," which means that when you get to the end of the sequence you return to the beginning and start over again. Good luck!

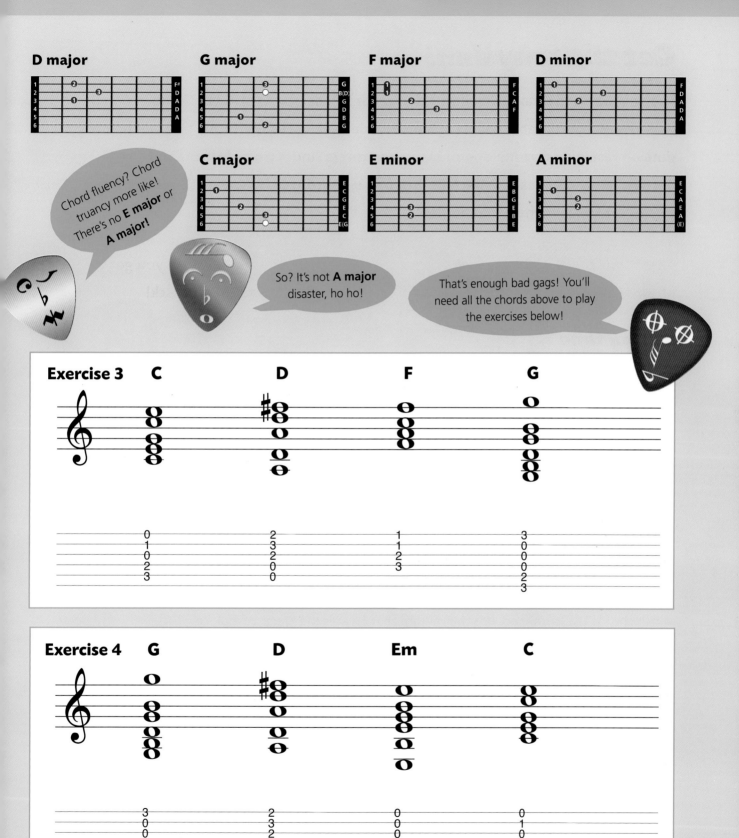

Get that rhythm!

Keeping time is the vital ability a musician needs to play a piece of music or accompany other musicians at exactly the right speed—without getting faster or slowing down. Many beginners find it one of the hardest skills to master, especially when they're concentrating on finding and playing the right chords!

Don't be put off if at first your playing sounds ragged or inconsistent. With practice, keeping time will soon become second nature!

Tempo time

Tempo is one of two elements of timing—the other is rhythm. The tempo refers to the specific speed of a piece of music, which is usually measured in "beats per minute" (bpm). Printed guitar music often shows a tempo instruction at the top of the page above the staffs. The example below indicates that a piece of music should be played at a tempo of 120 beats per minute.

$$\quad = 120$$

Feel the rhythm

Rhythm refers to the way in which notes are played or accented, and in which chords are strummed. It is the rhythm that creates the "feel" of a piece of music.

Time it right!

There are many different ways in which you can develop your sense of timing. Listen to the rhythm of your favourite records or CDs and try to strum the chords you know in time—this will give you a feel for different rhythms even if you can't yet play the song! Alternatively you can use a traditional metronome—a clockwork device that you can set to "click" at a specific tempo. A beat box can also work in this way.

GOING CLASSICAL?

Some written music is specified only in terms of a general tempo. Such instructions are traditionally indicated by the use of Italian names. This list shows the approximate range in beats per minute associated with each term (known as a "tempo mark").

Tempo mark	Description	BPM range
Grave	Very slow, serious	Below 40
Lento	Slow	40–55
Largo	Broad	45–65
Adagio	Slow (literally, at ease)	55–75
Andante	Walking speed	75–105
Moderato	Moderate speed	105–120
Allegro	Fast (literally, cheerful)	120–160
Vivace	Lively	150–170
Presto	Very fast	170–210
Prestissimo	As fast as possible	Above 210

Strict tempo?

If you play with a group of musicians, unless you are playing to a mechanical rhythm, you'll find the group will push and pull against the basic tempo at different points of a song. Far from being a sign of poor musicianship, the creation of a unique "feel" is the hallmark of a good band. You'll find you can play more urgently for drama, or quieten things down for a softer effect, depending on the mood you're trying to create.

Note values

Remember, a note played on the guitar has three basic characteristics:
pitch, **volume** and **duration**.

The **pitch** is governed by the fret position.

The **volume** is governed by how hard the string has been struck.

The **duration** is governed by how long the note is allowed to sustain.

In written music, the overall tempo is governed by how many beats should be played every minute—and an individual note takes its value in relation to the length of that beat.

Note divisions

The longest note value is a **whole note**, which is a note sustained for four beats. Subsequent notes may be halved in value until they reach a sixteenth of a beat—but don't panic, guitar players are rarely asked to play that quickly!

Each of the different types of note has its own unique symbol as it appears in written music, some of which are shown on the table below.

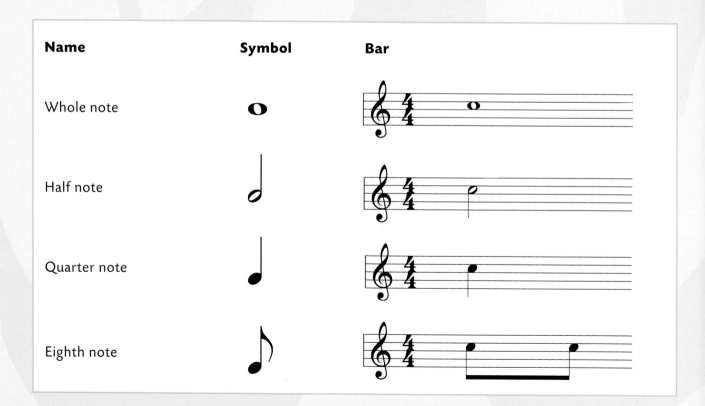

Name	Symbol	Bar
Whole note		
Half note		
Quarter note		
Eighth note		

Note values in practice

You may find it easier to understand note values by strumming the same sequence using chords with different time values. The following exercises use the open-string chords C major, A minor, E minor and G major. Remember them?

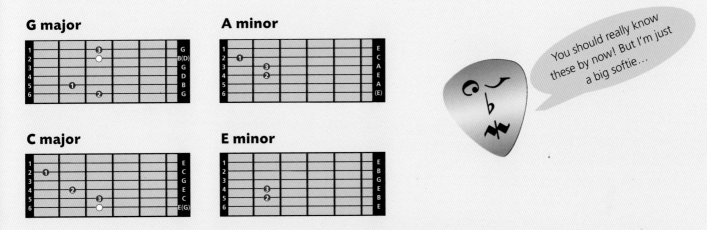

G major

A minor

C major

E minor

You should really know these by now! But I'm just a big softie...

As before, strike the strings of a chord in one sweeping movement, either with a pick or with the fingers of your right hand. Continuously count in seconds from one to four, emphasizing "one"—the first beat of the bar—each time. If you have a metronome or beat box, this will be easier.

Play whole-note chords!

The four chords in this exercise are made up from whole notes.

- Play C major on the first beat of the first bar. Sustain the chord while you count through four.
- Play A minor on the first beat of the second bar. Sustain the chord while you count through four.
- Play E minor on the first beat of the third bar. Sustain the chord while you count through four.
- Play G major on the first beat of the fourth bar. Sustain the chord while you count through four.

Or if you're feeling clever, follow the written music instructions below!

C   **Am**   **Em**   **G**

Note perfect!

OK, you've tried whole-note chords... but are you ready to try half notes, quarter notes and eighth notes?

Here we go… I can't wait to get battering those strings!

Play half-note chords!

Groups of notes that sustain for two beats are half notes. In this exercise each chord is played twice in every bar, once on the first beat and once on the third. Still not sure how to play the chords? You'll have to flick back a page—or use the chord finder, beginning on page 50.

- Play C major on the first beat of the first bar. Sustain the chord for two beats. On the count of three play the chord again. Sustain the chord while you count through to four.
- Play A minor on the first beat of the first bar. Sustain the chord for two beats. On the count of three play the chord again. Sustain the chord while you count through to four.
- Play E minor on the first beat of the first bar. Sustain the chord for two beats. On the count of three play the chord again. Sustain the chord while you count through to four.
- Play G major on the first beat of the first bar. Sustain the chord for two beats. On the count of three play the chord again. Sustain the chord while you count through to four.

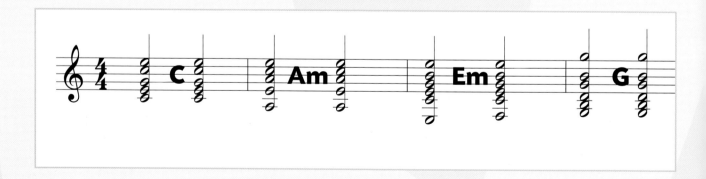

Play quarter-note chords!

This exercise halves the note value one stage further so that you play each chord four times, once on each beat. These chords are made up from quarter notes, and are sustained for one beat.

When you first try to play this exercise you may find that you have difficulty getting your left hand into position quickly enough. If this happens, start off by playing at a slower speed. You can also try playing this exercise using different right-hand techniques. If you are using a pick, start by using only downstrokes. After that you can begin to swap between downstrokes and upstrokes.

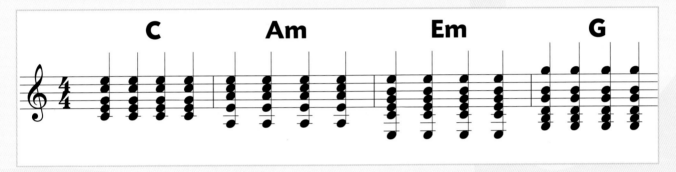

Play eighth-note chords!

This final exercise uses chords made up from quavers—notes that are sustained for half a beat.

This time around you must play two chords for each number that you count out. Therefore, to ensure that your strokes are of an equal value, try inserting the word "and" between each number—all you have to do is play on every half beat.

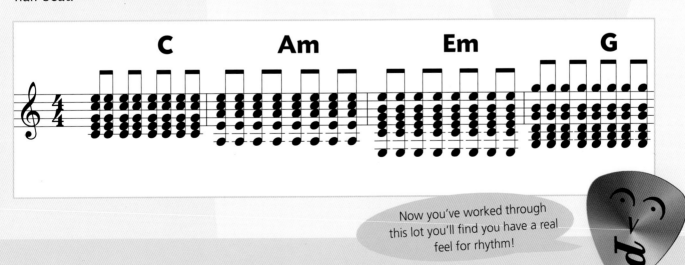

Now you've worked through this lot you'll find you have a real feel for rhythm!

Time signatures

When notes are written down, they are grouped together in small blocks called bars. Each bar contains a defined number of beats. It's easiest to explain this idea in terms of counting numbers out aloud: if you slowly and evenly count out "1–2–3–4–2–2–3–4–3–2–3–4–4–2–3–4" you have counted out four bars, with each single bar containing four beats.

Common time

You may have noticed that some of the written music you've seen on previous pages has begun with a pair of numbers, one sitting above the other on the staff to the left of the notes. These two numbers indicate the time signature of the piece of music. The number at the top tells you how many beats there are in each bar, and the bottom number tells you the time value of each of those beats.

In the example below there are four beats in the bar; each beat has a value of a quarter note, because it lasts for a quarter of the bar. This does not mean that each bar has to consist of four quarter notes, but simply that no matter how many notes are played in the bar, their total value must add up to the top figure, which in this case is four.

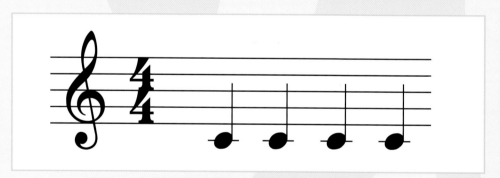

A piece of music which has four beats (quarter notes) in the bar is said to have a time signature of "four-four"—which is usually written in text as "4/4." Four-four time is far and away the most commonly used time signature—so much so, in fact, that it is also widely known as "common time."

Sometimes on written music you'll find common time is shortened on the staff as the letter "C," or in its more stylized form—𝄴.

Simple time

There are three basic time signatures:
- 2/4 time
- 3/4 time
- 4/4 time

These time signatures are known as "simple time." Four-bar groupings for each of these time signatures are shown below. Try counting along with each line of music, always accenting the first beat of each bar. The count for the four bars of 2/4, for example, would go "one—two—one—two—one—two—one—two."

Two-four time

There are two beats per bar. All of the beats are quarter notes.

Three-four time

There are three beats per bar. All of the beats are quarter notes.

Four-four time

There are four beats per bar. All of the beats are quarter notes.

With its unique, unmistakable feel, the 3/4 time signature is also known as "waltz time" or "triple" time and has three beats in each bar.

You will probably have noticed that the time signatures in 2/4 and 4/4 are essentially the same. However, the fact that the example in 2/4 would require twice as many bars to produce the same number of notes naturally alters the feel of the way the beats are counted.

Playing some tunes

Obviously, a great way of practicing the new chords and techniques you've been learning is to play them in songs. Here's an old folk tune you might recognize when you start playing it. If you're any good at singing, you can try singing along too—or ask someone to accompany you!

Dotted notes
A note followed by a dot means you lengthen that note by half its value. So, an eighth note with a dot in front of it means it is sustained for three-quarters of a beat instead of half a beat.

Sixteenth notes
A sixteenth note sustaines for a quarter of a beat. In this song you'll find them paired with dotted eighth notes—which means their total value is one beat.

Rests
This symbol tells you not to play anything for one quarter note—a single beat.

John Brown's Body

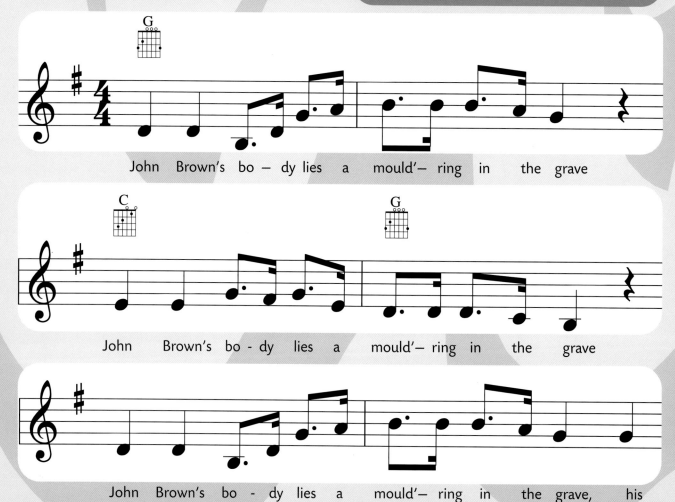

Whenever you see a chord or note tied across a bar line, the second note is NEVER played—it is simply an instruction to sustain the previous note of the last bar for its own value, PLUS the value of the second note.

Name that tune!

Here's a test to see if you're getting the hang of this guitar-playing thing! Over the next few pages you'll find some extracts from songs that have been around for donkey's years. Again, never mind that—just play them like exercises. Can you recognize the songs from these extracts? The answers are at the bottom of the page.

When you've practiced a few times, try playing them to your friends or family, and see if they recognize them. The chords they use are all simple ones. Can you work out how to play the rest of the songs? If you can't, chances are you can look them up in a beginner's book of guitar songs—good luck!

Don't forget to watch out for the time signatures—they're not all the same!

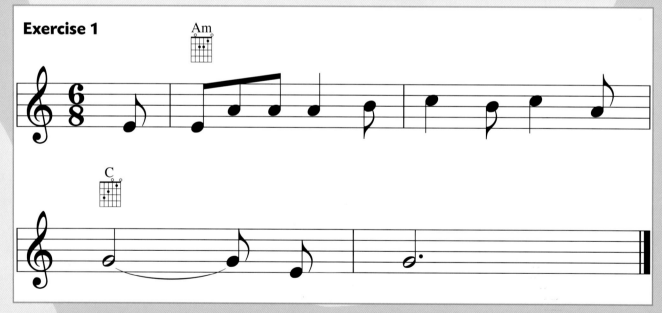

Exercise 1: When Johnny Comes Marching Home
Sing-along: When Johnny comes marching home again, hurrah! Hurrah!

Exercise 2

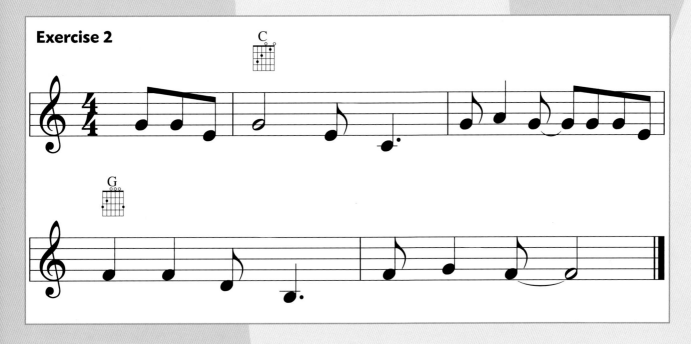

Exercise 3

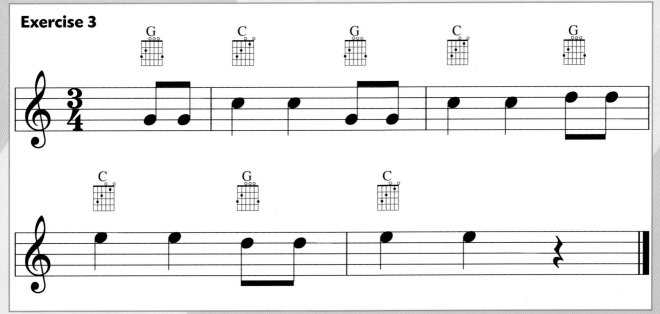

Exercise 2: He's Got the Whole World in His Hands
Sing-along: He's got the whole world in His hands, He's got the whole world in His hands!

Exercise 3: London's Burning
Sing-along: London's burning, London's burning, Fetch the engine, Fetch the engine!

Old Smokey

Here's another old folk song for you to try. It's in three-four time so if you want to count out the beat, remember that it repeats in cycles of three. Some of the cheerful words to this song are shown below, so you can sing along while you practice if you want!

2 Oh courting is pleasure and parting is grief
But a false-hearted lover is worse than a thief!

3 A thief will just rob you of all that you save
But a false-hearted lover will lead to the grave

4 The grave will decay you and turn you to dust
Not one in a million a poor boy (girl) can trust

5 They'll kiss you and squeeze you and tell you more lies
Than the rain drops from heaven or stars from the skies

6 It's raining and hailing this cold stormy night
Your horses can't travel for the moon gives no light

7 So put up your horses and give them some hay
And come sit beside me as long as you stay

8 My horses aren't hungry, they don't want your hay
I'm anxious to leave so I'll be on my way

9 On top of old Smokey, all covered with snow
I lost my true lover by courting too slow!

What next?

Obviously, there's a whole lot more to playing the guitar than we can show you in this book. But we hope we've got you past the first few playing hurdles and fired up your enthusiasm. So... what next?

The chordtastic chord finder!

Knowing a whole range of different chords is probably the most useful capability that a guitarist can acquire. It also provides composers and songwriters with a wide range of raw materials, from which songs can be created.

The Chord Finder on the following pages is a useful reference guide, showing you how to play a whole bunch of chords. Although some of them will by now be familiar to you, others we've avoided so far because they are not simple open-string chords.

The most difficult of these require you to hold your first finger over more than one string—and sometimes all six strings. These are called "barre chords." By following the chord diagrams in the same way as the open-string chords, with practice you should be able to play them.

You'll also notice that the voicing of each chord appears with two alternative positions—for when you're feeling more confident. After all, as far as playing goes, from here, the sky's the limit!

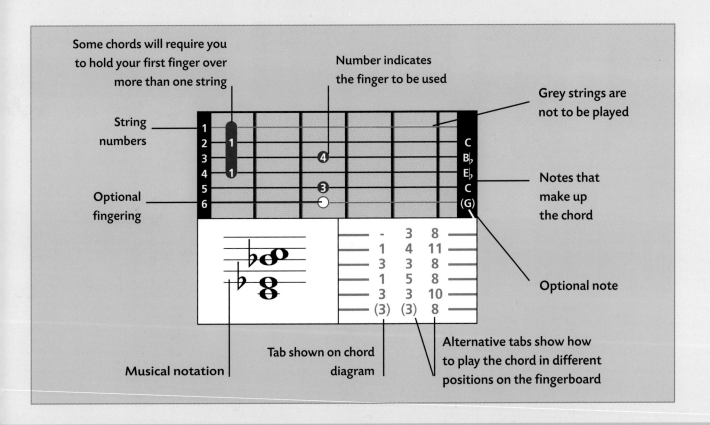

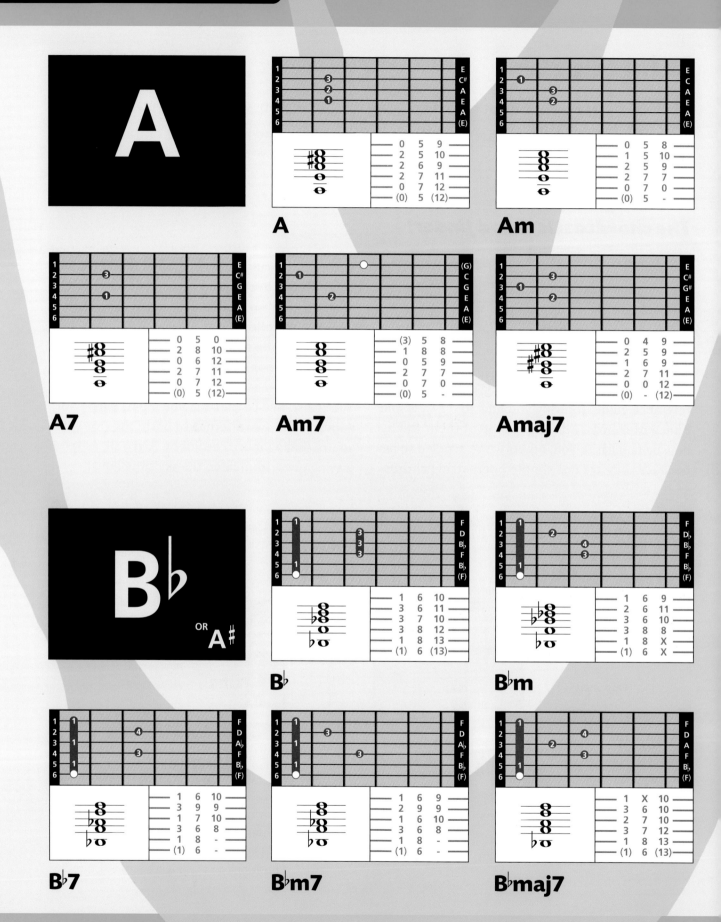

B

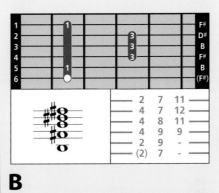

B

Bm

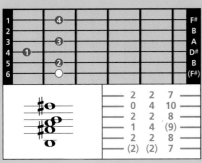

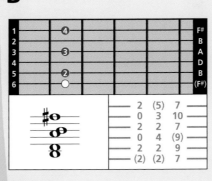

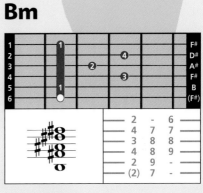

B7

Bm7

Bmaj7

C

C

Cm

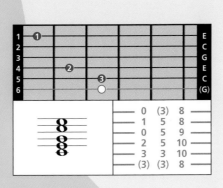

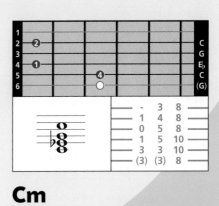

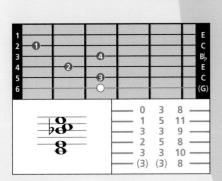

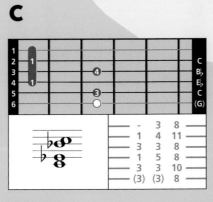

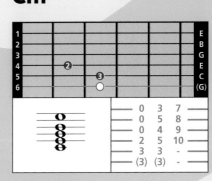

C7

Cm7

Cmaj7

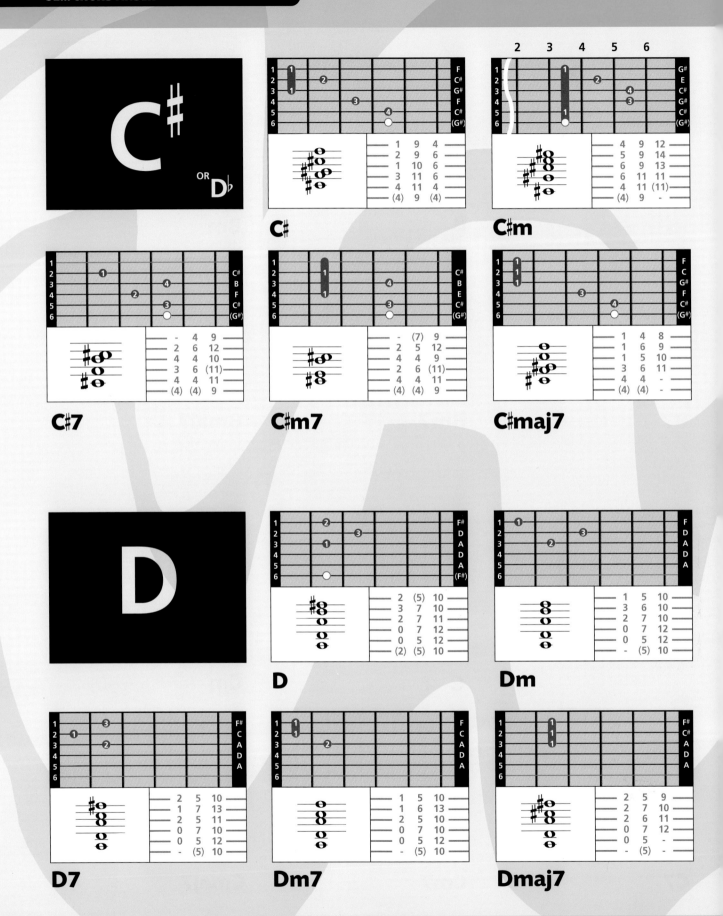

C#

C# C#m

C#7 C#m7 C#maj7

D

D Dm

D7 Dm7 Dmaj7

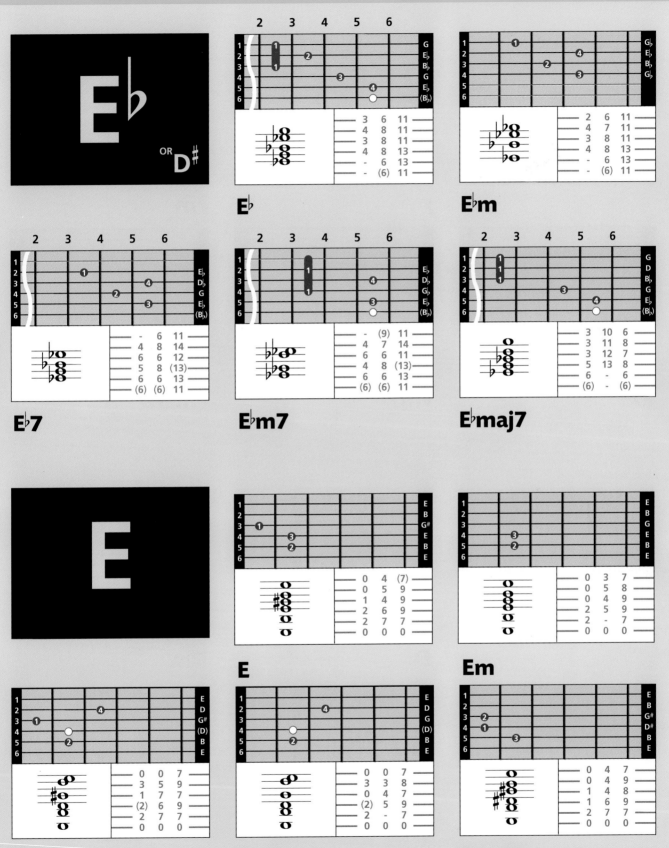

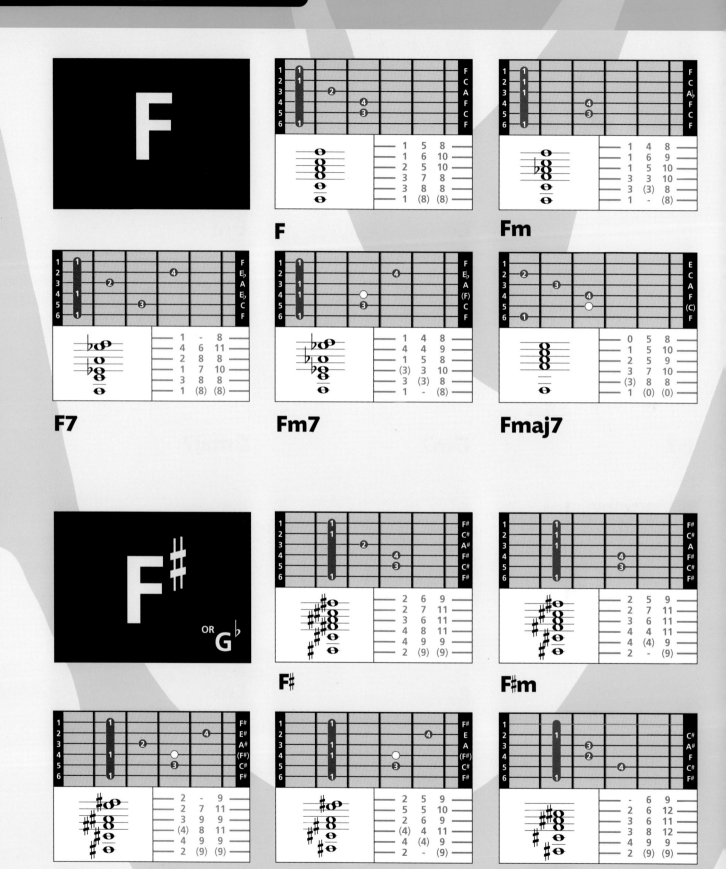

F

F

Fm

F7

Fm7

Fmaj7

F#
OR Gb

F#

F#m

F#7

F#m7

F#maj7

G

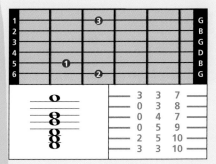

G

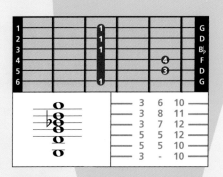

Gm

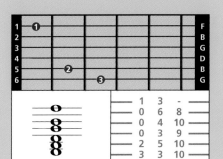

G7

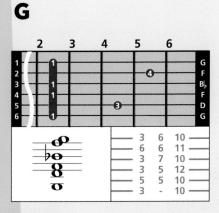

Gm7

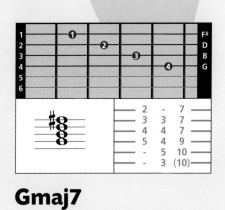

Gmaj7

A♭

OR **G#**

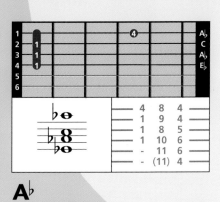

A♭

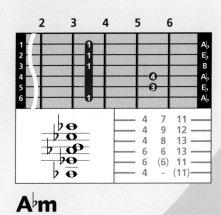

A♭m

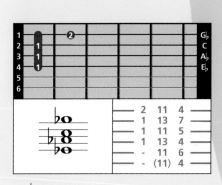

A♭7

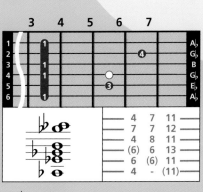

A♭m7

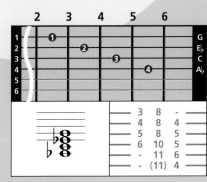

A♭maj7

Special effects!

Electronic effects units—whether they're simple foot pedals or costly digital multi-effect units—let the guitarist produce a huge range of sounds. Quite simply, for most types of music, effects are now essential.

Hot-foot it!

The simplest and cheapest way of getting an electronic effect is to buy a plug-in foot pedal. Most of the commonly heard effects—such as delay, chorus, phasing, and flanging—can be created in this way, and they're extremely easy to use. All you need is an additional guitar lead. The effect is inserted between the guitar and amplifier, the guitar is plugged into the "In" socket on the effect, using one lead, and the second lead is connected between the "Out" socket on the effect and the amplifier. The diagram below should make it clear.

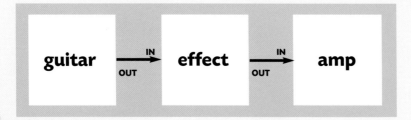

What to get?

There are plenty of effects to choose from. Here are some of the most useful:

Reverb
Short for reverberation, this adds warmth and atmosphere to the original sound, producing a feeling of space.

Delay
Delay adds a very noticeable echo to the original sound. You can change the length of the delay to achieve different effects—basically it sounds like there's two of you playing, one always a little way behind the other.

Chorus
A kind of very fast delay, chorus beefs up a "thin" guitar sound so it sounds much fuller—almost like you're playing along with someone else.

Distortion
One of the most famous effects, this distorts the clean guitar sound, adding fuzz and a feeling of crackling power... just watch your ears!

PLAYING IN THE HOME

For the electric guitarist, practicing in the home can be a bit of a nightmare. If you crank your amp up too high, your family and neighbors will be quick to complain (and you can damage your hearing too). One solution is to use a small practice amplifier, usually of less than five watts in power, that has the features of a standard guitar amplifier. The best-quality models are designed to create an excellent sound at low volumes.

Another popular solution is to practice using headphones. A number of multi-effect guitar pedals come with headphone sockets, so you don't even necessarily need an amplifier—the sound won't be particularly great, but you'll still be able to hear yourself.

Or, if you own a multitrack recorder (see page 60) you can plug your guitar and effects into that and then connect the multitrack safely to your hi-fi—so long as your hi-fi has a "line in" socket at the back.

One last point: NEVER be tempted to take the amplifier output and plug it directly into your hi-fi—if you ever want to listen to another CD, anyway!

If you're not sure which effects unit to buy, ask if you can try out a few down your local music store—or ask for a demonstration.

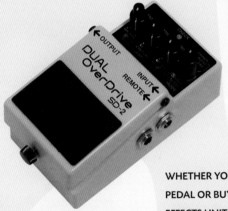

WHETHER YOU GO FOR ONE PEDAL OR BUY A MULTI-EFFECTS UNIT, IT'S GREAT FUN TO EXPLORE DIFFERENT SOUNDS.

Keep it clean!

Your guitar isn't just a thing to be played, it's an instrument that will only sound its best if it's well looked after. Remember, a good guitar can be an investment that, if well-cared for, will increase in value over the years.

Fight the filth!

When cleaning your guitar, avoid those cleaning agents that contain silicone or wax, as they can sometimes give the instrument an unpleasant, sticky feel and affect the coloring. NEVER use abrasive cleaning fluids, as these will damage the finish. If in doubt, ask the store that sold you your guitar what will be best.

Cleaning the strings
Keeping your strings clean not only makes the guitar feel more pleasant to play, but it can make the strings last a good deal longer. The most effective cleaning method is to take a dry, lint-free cloth, pass it between the strings and fingerboard, and drag it the full length of the strings between the bridge and the nut.

Cleaning the fingerboard
Fretboards with a synthetic varnish can be cleaned in the same way as the body. Many guitars have oiled ebony or rosewood fingerboards. These should be given a good cleaning every time you change the strings (see below). A neat trick here is to apply some lemon oil to the wood and leave it for five minutes before wiping it off with a dry cloth. This cleans the fingerboard, maintains its feel, and keeps the wood from drying out.

Cleaning the frets
Dirt from the fingers often builds along the edge of the frets. This should be carefully removed with a gently pointed object, such as a toothpick.

Hardware
Keeping the guitar's metal parts clean is the most effective way of preventing rusting. Ask your music store for advice on which cleaner to use.

SPECIALLY MADE
CLEANING AGENTS ARE
WIDELY AVAILABLE.

Strings on the earliest guitars were usually made from the intestines of sheep!

UGH! That doesn't **baa** thinking about!

An open and shut case!

The best way of keeping your guitar clean and safe is to store it in a specially made case when it's not being used. These come in a wide variety of shapes and sizes. The most basic cases are made from padded plastic or fabric, and zip around the outside of the guitar. Although these are very cheap, to be honest it's just as effective to wrap your guitar up in an old thick blanket—if less neat and tidy.

The sturdiest cases have a hard shell, and the insides are padded to keep the instrument in place, and lined with fake fur to protect the body finish. Most of these are ideal for everyday protection.

CHANGING STRINGS

Different guitars have different string-fixing mechanisms—both at the bridge and headstock—all of which require slightly different string-changing techniques. In all cases, whenever you fit new strings they need to be "stretched." To do this, pull the string a few inches away from the fretboard and then release it. If the pitch has dropped, retune it and repeat. Keep doing this until the string stays broadly in tune.

How often you change your strings is down to you. Some professional players restring every time they perform or record—but others leave strings in place for years, or until they break. Whatever you do, if you put on a new set of strings, they will need to be "worn in"—a few hours of playing should do this nicely.

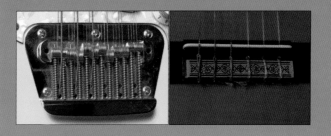

Don't store your guitar in the loft or basement, or close to radiators and hot water pipes—this can warp your guitar and ruin both its sound and appearance!

Home and away

You're practicing the guitar because you want to be a musician. Maybe you want to write your own songs, or maybe you'll be happy playing other people's. Whichever, at some point you'll probably want to record your work—and maybe hook up with others to start a band!

Home recording

Recording yourself playing has a lot going for it—no matter how good you are. If you record yourself practicing, you can listen back and hear your mistakes; this might be a painful experience but it will help you work out what parts of your playing you need to focus on. If there's a tape recorder in your home with an in-built microphone, there's nothing more you really need—get going!

WEARING HEADPHONES WHILE YOU PRACTICE WILL BE APPRECIATED BY FAMILY AND NEIGHBORS!

As your playing improves, you may want to start recording proper songs. A multitrack recorder, while quite expensive, will be a great help to you here. Unlike a stereo recorder, you can record a number of separate pieces of music (or tracks) on the same piece of tape. And you can record in stages, gradually building up your song—put the first verse on track one, stop, play it back and then record the chorus on track two, and so on. More and more people—including some really famous names—are now using their home computers to record their own multitrack music.

The only downside is that multitracks can make you lazy—there's no need to get the perfect performance every time. But you can also use them to accompany yourself—maybe adding some lead guitar over some strumming. And the only other way to achieve that effect is to join a band...

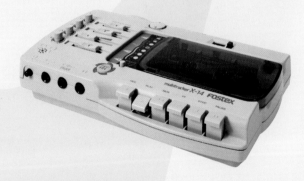

THERE ARE MANY QUITE AFFORDABLE MULTITRACK RECORDERS AROUND—AND YOU CAN ALWAYS CHECK FOR SECONDHAND BARGAINS!

Group therapy!

Playing with other people who share your taste in music can be great fun. Think about what sort of music you want to play, and what instruments will be needed. If you and a friend both play guitar, perhaps one of you could try singing. Or perhaps you could find a bass player and drummer to beef up your sound. Or perhaps you could find a keyboard player and play along to their beat box instead. The great thing is, there are no rules in music—it's all up to you! If your school has an orchestra or music club, that might be a good place to make contacts. Or you could ask your music teacher for advice.

Finding a place to meet and rehearse can be a problem if your band is too big for a bedroom. If your school can provide a place to play, great— otherwise perhaps you could get together in your garage. If you're a bit noisy, and your music requires a singer, you might get away with plugging a microphone into a spare channel on your amplifier, although it probably won't sound too great!

You may find that you can't hear yourself playing very well either, but whatever you do, DON'T turn up your own volume to compensate—everyone else will copy you, and you and your neighbors will be deafened!

Whatever you do, and wherever your guitar-playing takes you, the important thing is to always have fun…

Practice can be a pain, but it'll be worth it in the end when you can play whatever you like! **GOOD LUCK!**

Glossary

Acoustic Guitar
Guitar that can be played without using amplification.

Action
The height between the strings and the frets on the fretboard. The higher the action, the harder it becomes to fret notes.

Bridge
A mechanical device fitted to the body of an electric guitar that supports the strings and controls their height and length. On an acoustic guitar, the part into which the strings are set.

Chord
The sound of three or more notes played at the same time. Two notes played simultaneously can create a chordal effect. although this is technically known as an interval.

Chorus
Electronic delay effect that simulates more than one instrument playing the same part. Variations in pitch and time can be used to create a richer, thicker effect.

Delay
Digital simulation of natural reflected sounds, such as echo.

Distortion
Electronic effect created by heavily boosting the volume in the preamp stage of the amplifier. Can also be achieved using external effects units.

Electric guitar
A solid-bodied guitar that must be plugged into an external amplifier.

Electro-acoustic guitar
A guitar that can be played acoustically or plugged into an external amplifier.

Feedback
A sound produced when amplified sound from a loudspeaker causes a string to vibrate.

Fingerpicking
Right-hand playing technique in which the strings are plucked by individual fingers.

Fret
Metal strips placed at intervals along the fingerboard.

Headstock
The uppermost part of the guitar neck, where the machine heads are mounted.

Machine head
Mechanical device for controlling the tension, and therefore pitch, of a string.

Nut
The string supports positioned at the top of the fingerboard.

Octave
An interval of 12 half steps. Doubling the sound frequency of any note has the effect of increasing the pitch by an octave.

Pedals
Foot-controlled electronic units placed between the output of the guitar and the input of the amplifier, which can be used to process the sound in a variety of different ways.

Pick
Object used for striking the guitar strings—usually made from plastic. Also sometimes known as a plectrum.

Pickups
Electro-magnetic transducers that convert string vibration into electrical impulses, which are then amplified and played back through a loudspeaker.

Soundboard
The front of the guitar on which the bridge is mounted.

Tempo
The speed at which a piece of music is played. Usually measured in beats per minute (bpm).

Time signature
Two numbers shown at the beginning of a piece of music, indicating both the number of beats, and their value, within a bar.

Some useful websites

www.entertainment.howstuffworks.com/guitar.htm
This is a cool place to go if you want to find out a load more about your guitar and how it works, whether it's acoustic or electric!

www.rockhall.com
Explore the rock 'n' roll hall of fame and get the lowdown on guitar heroes of the past and present... and find out what was happening today in rock history!

www.fender.com
The official sites of the world-famous Fender guitars and amplifiers. As well as online catalogs and price guides you'll find news, a discussion forum and loads of info on the gear and on the artists currently using it!

www.houlston.freeserve.co.uk
This free site has lots of musical exercises in Tab style and loads of cool guitar info. But best of all is the online tuner—you can tune up to an MP3 file of each note!

www.guitarnoise.com
This site bills itself as an online guitar college. It has some interesting and accessible lessons that could help improve your technique—and loads more!

www.classicbands.com
Did you know that Shania Twain's real name is Eileen Regina Edwards? For loads more amazing trivia on the American music scene check out this site.

Index